21st Century
Basic Skills
Library

BABY ZOO ANIMALS
CHEETAHS

by Katie Marsico

Cherry Lake Publishing • Ann Arbor, Michigan

3

CHERRY
LAKE
Publishing

Published in the United States of America
by Cherry Lake Publishing
Ann Arbor, Michigan
www.cherrylakepublishing.com

Content Adviser: Dr. Stephen S. Ditchkoff, Professor of Wildlife Sciences,
Auburn University, Auburn, Alabama

Photo Credits: Cover and pages 1, 16, and 20; ©Francois van Heerden/
Shutterstock, Inc.; page 4, ©Mark Beckwith/Shutterstock, Inc.; pages 6
and 8, ©Duncan Noakes/Dreamstime.com; page 10, ©Jason Prince/
Shutterstock, Inc.; page 12, ©Thoron/Dreamstime.com; page 14, ©Keith
Barlow/Dreamstime.com; page 18, ©Albie Venter/Shutterstock, Inc.

Library of Congress Cataloging-in-Publication Data
Marsico, Katie, 1980–
Cheetahs / by Katie Marsico.
     p. cm. — (21st century basic skills library) (Baby zoo animals)
  Includes bibliographical references and index.
  ISBN 978-1-61080-453-0 (lib. bdg.) — ISBN 978-1-61080-540-7 (e-book) —
ISBN 978-1-61080-627-5 (pbk.)
1. Cheetah—Infancy—Juvenile literature. 2. Zoo animals—Infancy—
Juvenile literature. I. Title.
  SF408.6.C49M37 2013
  599.75'9—dc23   2012001724

Cherry Lake Publishing would like to acknowledge
the work of The Partnership for 21st Century Skills.
Please visit www.21stcenturyskills.org for more information.

Printed in the United States of America
Corporate Graphics Inc.
July 2012
CLFA11

TABLE OF CONTENTS

5   **Cubs of Fast Cats**

13   **A Cheetah's Day**

19   **All Grown Up!**

22   Find Out More

22   Glossary

23   Home and School Connection

24   Fast Facts

24   Index

24   About the Author

Cubs of Fast Cats

Cheetahs are the world's fastest land **mammals.**

They can run 70 miles (113 kilometers) per hour!

Most cheetahs live in Africa. Others are found in zoos across the globe.

Cheetahs give birth to between two and eight cubs at a time.

Baby cheetahs are helpless when they are born.

They are blind and furry. Longer hair covers their backs, necks, and heads.

It will take time for the cubs to move as fast as their parents.

Cheetah cubs drink their mother's milk at first.

Zookeepers feed them meat after about 2 months.

A Cheetah's Day

Cheetahs are most active during the day.

This is when they hunt **prey**.

Cheetahs at the zoo eat ground beef and chicken.

Zookeepers play with cheetah cubs. They tie a toy to a long stick.

They drag it along the ground. Cubs chase after it.

Mother cheetahs **communicate** with their cubs. They warn the cubs of danger.

Cheetahs purr and hiss. They might even sound like chirping birds!

All Grown Up!

Wild cheetahs stay with their mothers for about 18 months.

They are sometimes together for more or less time at zoos.

Female cheetahs are adults when they are about 2 years old. Then they are ready to have babies.

Then zookeepers welcome new cheetah cubs!

Find Out More

BOOK

Randall, Henry. *Cheetahs*. New York: PowerKids Press, 2011.

WEB SITE

The San Diego Zoo Kids—African Cheetah
http://kids.sandiegozoo.org/animals/mammals/african-cheetah
Check out this site for a video, photos, and fast facts about cheetahs.

Glossary

cheetahs (CHEE-tuhz) large, spotted cats in Africa and Asia

communicate (kuh-MYOO-ni-kate) share information, ideas, or feelings

mammals (MA-muhlz) warm-blooded animals that have hair or fur, give birth to live babies, and make milk to feed their young

prey (PRAY) animals that are hunted and killed by other animals for food

zookeepers (ZOO-kee-purz) workers who take care of animals at zoos

Home and School Connection

Use this list of words from the book to help your child become a better reader. Word games and writing activities can help beginning readers reinforce literacy skills.

a	born	female	land	of	they
about	can	feed	less	old	this
across	chase	first	like	or	tie
active	cheetah	for	live	others	time
adults	cheetahs	found	long	parents	to
Africa	chicken	furry	longer	per	together
after	chirping	give	mammals	play	toy
along	communicate	globe	meat	prey	two
and	covers	ground	might	purr	warn
are	cubs	hair	miles	ready	welcome
as	danger	have	milk	run	when
at	day	heads	months	sometimes	wild
babies	drag	helpless	more	sound	will
baby	drink	hiss	most	stay	with
backs	during	hour	mother	stick	world's
beef	eat	hunt	mother's	take	years
between	eight	in	mothers	the	zoo
birds	even	is	move	their	zookeepers
birth	fast	it	necks	them	zoos
blind	fastest	kilometers	new	then	

Fast Facts

Habitat: Grasslands
Range: Mostly in Africa, with small numbers living in parts of Asia
Average Length: 3.5 to 4.5 feet (1.1 to 1.4 meters), with a tail between 25 and 32 inches (64 to 81 centimeters) long
Average Weight: 77 to 143 pounds (35 to 65 kilograms)
Life Span: About 10 to 12 years

Index

adulthood, 21
Africa, 7
antelope, 13
births, 7, 9
communication, 17
cubs, 7, 9, 11, 15, 17, 21

danger, 17
food, 11, 13
hair, 9
hunting, 13
milk, 11
mothers, 11, 17, 19

playing, 15
prey, 13
speeds, 5, 9
zookeepers, 11, 15,
zoos, 7, 13, 19

About the Author

Katie Marsico is the author of more than 100 children's and young-adult reference books. She likes the fact that she can watch cheetahs at the zoo without worrying about having to outrun them.

24